THE INTERNATIONAL DEBT CRISIS

Wendy Davies

Rourke Enterprises, Inc.
Vero Beach, Florida 32964

World Issues

Endangered Wildlife
Food or Famine?
International Terrorism
Nuclear Weapons
Population Growth
Refugees
The Arms Trade
The Energy Crisis
The Environment
The International Debt Crisis
The International Drug Trade
World Health

Text © 1989 Rourke Enterprises, Inc.

All rights reserved. No part of this book may be reproduced or utilized in any form or by any means, electronic or mechanical, including photocopying and recording, or by any information storage and retrieval system without permission in writing from the publisher.

Cover: Main picture: The dealing room of an international bank. Inset: Children in the slums of Rio de Janiero, Brazil
Frontispiece: Poor housing in Peru

Library of Congress Cataloging-in-Publication Data

Davies, Wendy.
    The international debt crisis/Wendy Davies.
      p. cm. – (World issues)
    Bibliography: p.
    Includes index.
    Summary: Explains the world's financial system and how it functions and the problems created by the increasing debts owed by developing nations.
    ISBN 0-86592-076-1
    1. Debts, External – Developing countries – Juvenile literature.
2. Developing countries – Economic conditions – Juvenile literature.
[1. Debts, External – Developing countries.   2. Developing countries–   Economic conditions.]   I. Title   II. Series: World issues (Vero Beach, Fla.)
HJ8899.D38 1988
336.3'435'091724 – dc19   88–18408
                                                    CIP
                                                      AC

Manufactured in Italy

Contents

1. Money makes the world go around　6
2. Who holds the world's purse strings?　14
3. Whose crisis?　20
4. Debt management　32
5. The need for change　39

Glossary　45

Books to read　46

Index　47

1 Money makes the world go around

If you borrow money from your parents, you may arrange to pay it back in small amounts over a number of weeks or months. If your parents borrow money from a bank, they will also arrange to pay it back over a period of time. The difference is that they will be charged *interest*. This is a percentage of the amount they have borrowed that is added onto the original loan and continues to be added until the loan and the amount owed in interest is paid off. If the interest rate is high it can substantially increase the total amount that has to be paid, so unless the repayments are increased the debt grows instead of getting smaller.

When countries borrow money from foreign banks or governments they have even greater problems repaying the debt because they usually have to repay it in the foreign currency they borrowed it in. So, if a Latin American country borrows from an American bank, it then has to earn enough dollars by selling goods to the United States or another Western nation to repay the loan. This affects the way its economy is run and the livelihoods of the people in the country.

The world's financial system is extremely complex. It is difficult for us to understand in detail how it works, but we can appreciate how it seems to be heavily weighted in favor of the developed nations and against the poorer, developing nations. We can learn about how this imbalance came to exist and the effects it has on the developing countries. The burden of debt that many developing countries bear has a human cost as well as a financial one, and it is at the root of many of the world's problems. Poverty, hunger and sickness have increased as a result of the enormous payments the governments of these countries have to make to Western banks and financial institutions in return for money they have borrowed.

The problems created by the increasing debts of the developing nations can only be fully understood when we look at some of the background to the world's trading and financial system.

The Wall Street Crash

Until the end of the 1920s it was assumed that the world's financial system was fundamentally sound. This assumption was shaken for all time by the events of 1929 and the 1930s. These came to be known as the Great Crash and the Great Depression.

The 1920s was a profitable time for bankers and financiers in the United States. Business was expanding rapidly both within the United States and abroad, and there was a great deal of money to be made from stocks and shares. The banks sent thousands of agents all over the country, persuading the American public to buy shares in enterprises in Europe and Latin America. Between 1924 and 1928 American loans flowing into Europe and Latin America averaged $1.3 billion a year. These ventures were risky but could be highly profitable. The banks were often careless about checking the soundness of the investments and unscrupulous about lending to repressive and corrupt regimes.

The peak of this great financial boom came in 1929. People became rich overnight as the value of their shares rose like bubbles in a glass of champagne. But the day came when the champagne went flat.

On October 24, 1929, the great Wall Street Crash began, and 13 million shares were sold at falling prices. Within three weeks share values had fallen by half, and people flocked to the

Right: *During the Depression that followed the Wall Street Crash, unemployment rose and many people became destitute.*

banks to withdraw their money. In 1930 the Bank of the United States was forced to close its doors, wiping out the savings of 500,000 depositors – the biggest bank failure in American history. By the end of 1933, nearly 7,000 banks had closed and millions of people had lost their savings.

The entire country was plunged into chaos. As the Depression deepened, unemployment rose sharply. More and more people were thrown out of their homes as they were unable to pay their rent, and poverty and hunger became widespread. There were demonstrations, hunger marches and riots all over the country. In 1932, the low point of the Depression, industrial production sank to one-third and share prices to one-ninth of the 1929 level. Twenty thousand destitute war veterans marched on Congress and were driven away by the army with tear gas, bayonets and tanks.

The entire pattern of international trade was disrupted by the collapse of investment from the United States. The United States government also raised tariffs on imported goods to encourage Americans to buy American-made products. Latin American countries were therefore unable to increase their exports to the United States and could not raise the money to keep up interest payments. Many of them had to default on their loans.

Unemployed demonstrators in 1930 in Union Square, New York, running away from police armed with tear gas.

Toward a new crisis

Fifty years after the events of the Wall Street Crash and its aftermath, further troubles hit the world financial system. This has generally been called the debt crisis. The immediate causes of the debt crisis lie in the events of the 1970s. In the 1950s and 1960s bank lending had not played any significant part in financing the development of Third World countries. Investment by foreign businesses and government aid had meant that loans were not necessary. Then, in the 1970s, the commercial banks stepped in.

They were able to do this because of the oil crisis. In 1973 the oil-producing countries doubled and then redoubled the price of oil. This hit the rest of the world hard, particularly,

In 1973 oil prices rose sharply, increasing the problems of non-oil-producing nations and, in particular, of developing countries.

of course, developing countries that simply did not have the money to pay for oil bills four times higher than they had been before. They began to look around for loans.

Meanwhile, the oil-exporting countries were piling up huge sums of money. They deposited their increased income with the commercial banks of the United States, Western Europe and Japan, which in turn looked for new borrowers. All of a sudden the banks were extremely anxious to lend money to those developing countries that they considered to be creditworthy.

> Through the main entrance more bankers are swarming in, whose roving eyes suggest a very practical purpose. ... Across there a pack of Japanese bankers ... is converging on a finance minister. Along the corridor a grave-looking French banker looks as if he is in full pursuit of new African prey. ... As they pursue their prey down the escalators, up the elevators, along the upstairs corridors into the suites, they cannot conceal their anxiety to do business. For these men who look as if they might have been trained to say No from their childhood are actually trying to sell loans.
>
> (Anthony Sampson describing the pursuit of Third World finance ministers by bankers at an IMF meeting)

The new loans were very welcome. Unlike traditional aid from Western governments there were no awkward conditions attached; the countries receiving them did not have to use the money to provide basic necessities such as health care and education. On the whole, the borrowers had a free hand to use the money however they liked. Some countries embarked on prestigious development projects: establishing new industries and building dams, airports, roads and hotels. But the other difference was that the rates of interest payable on the loans were floating rather than fixed. In other words, they could rise or fall, and there-

A nuclear power station under construction. Some of the developing countries that borrowed extensively from Western banks used large sums out of their national budget for expensive, over-ambitious projects.

fore the amount that the borrowers were expected to repay each year could be increased or decreased.

Western governments were happy to let the banks take on the major role of providing finance for development. Their own aid budgets were being cut in "real" terms (that is, in comparison with the cost of living) and it was convenient to be able, to a certain extent, to hand over the responsibility. They made no attempt to control bank lending, believing that the world financial system would control itself.

At first interest rates were fairly low and the debtor countries had no great difficulty in keeping up payments. Then in 1979, mainly because of the revolution in Iran, the price of oil doubled again. Western governments began to adopt harsh policies to reduce inflation, including limiting imports to protect their own manufacturing industries. This made things extremely tough for developing countries since the only way they could repay their debts was to make more money by increasing the amount they earned from selling goods to Western countries. To make matters worse, prices paid for Third World commodities, which had been steadily falling throughout the 1970s, dropped even more dramatically. Interest rates rose sky-high. Developing countries were therefore earning much less, while paying out much more on their floating-rate loans. Eventually the strain became too great.

After the revolution in Iran in which the Shah was replaced by a government under Ayatollah Khomeini, oil prices rose partly as a result of the disruption to production of Iranian oil.

Commodity prices 1970-84

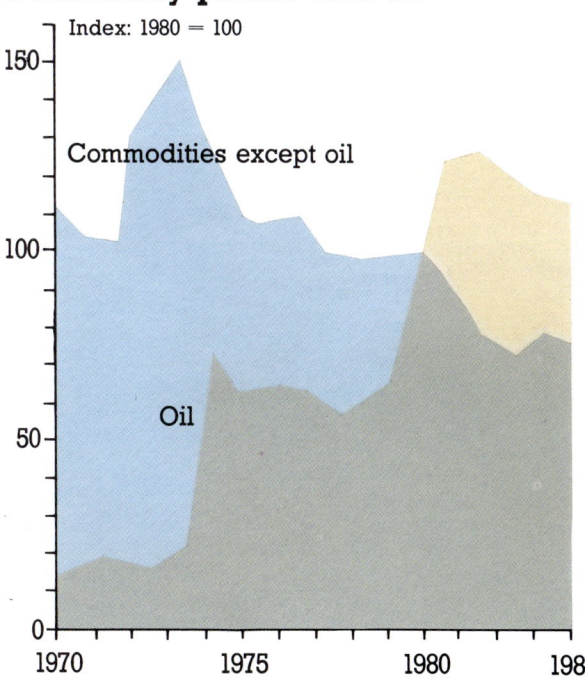

11

The crisis breaks

In August 1982 Mexico, which owed over $80 billion, announced that it could no longer keep up with repayments. Its central bank had only enough money to pay for twelve minutes' worth of imports! The country declared a halt on all repayments for ninety days, during which time they hoped to be able to work out new ways of repaying the money they owed.

This was the moment many bankers had privately dreaded. By August 1982 a total of $478 billion was owed by developing countries to commercial banks in the United States, Western Europe and Japan. The biggest debtors were the countries that were rapidly building up their industries, many of them Latin American. Among these were four "debt giants": Mexico, Brazil, Argentina and Venezuela. Among them they were responsible for 80 percent of Latin America's debt. By the end of 1982 these four countries and Chile seemed unable to keep up with repayments.

It is normal practice for banks to lend out more money than they actually possess. This is because the amount of money they are considered to have includes money owed to them. By the time of Mexico's announcement in 1982 some of the banks had lent more than twice as much as they possessed to Latin America. They were obviously extremely vulnerable to any of the major debtors falling behind with repayments, or possibly refusing to pay altogether.

The prospect of a major debtor defaulting and other countries following suit was a frightening one for the banks. There was the fear that leading banks could be bankrupted and that the entire international banking system could collapse. The creditors therefore rushed to prop up the system and to find ways of putting themselves out of danger.

Over the next few years measures were taken by creditors and, usually unwillingly, by debtors to control the crisis. Developing countries suffered great hardships in their efforts to adjust their economies and continue to pay the interest on their debts.

The debts continued to grow year by year and although the global financial system did not collapse, several countries did suspend or limit their payments. By 1987 the total foreign debt of developing countries had risen to a staggering level: well over $1,000 billion.

It may seem that the debt crisis is not your concern, but even your local bank is involved in loans to developing countries and could therefore help solve the problem.

In February 1987 Brazil, which owed more money than any other country, announced a suspension of payments on a large proportion of its debts. This was the biggest financial moratorium in history.

Third World responsibility

Western banks and governments must take their share of responsibility for the crisis, but they are not the only actors in the drama. Responsibility also lies with the governments of debtor countries and with members of the wealthy privileged groups within those

Many Latin American debtor countries have spent large sums of money on sophisticated weapons. For example, while Argentina was under military rule from 1976 to 1983 its foreign debt rose by $30 billion.

societies. Much of the money borrowed went on projects that did not benefit ordinary people. In some cases it was spent on armaments rather than on development. Huge sums of money were sent abroad by wealthy people, who were attracted by the high interest rates they got for their investments. It has been estimated that between 1979 and 1982, $60 billion left Mexico, Argentina and Venezuela alone.

2 Who holds the world's purse strings?

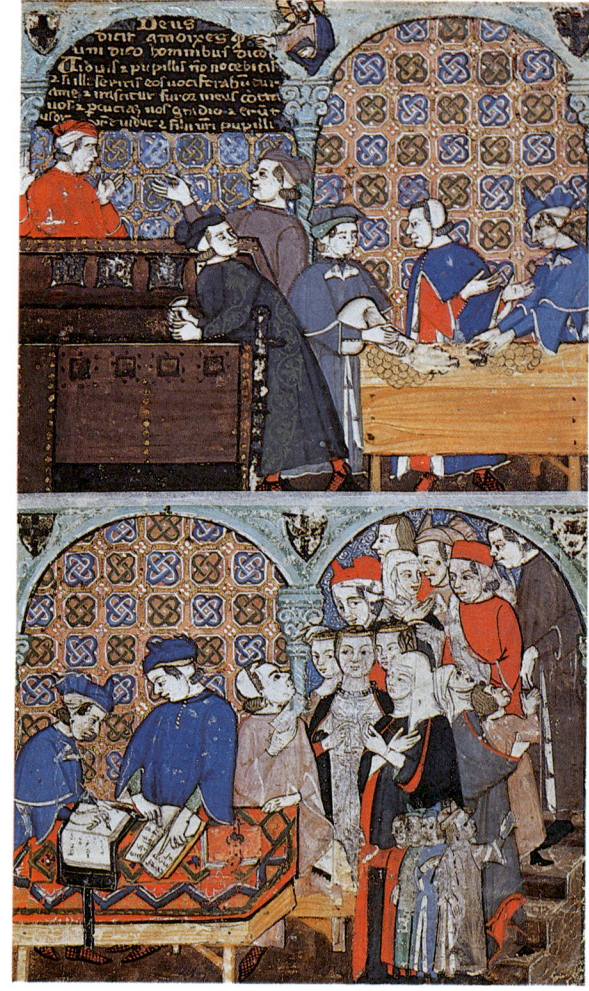

An Italian bank in 1380. The counting house is shown at the top, while the lower panel shows the customers lining up for their loans.

Debt and development

Most people in the West think that the problems of debt and poverty belong to remote parts of the world and many believe that developing countries simply do not know how to run their affairs and their economies properly. These are mistaken views. As Anthony Sampson has pointed out in *The Money Lenders*:

> Every country, of course, was once a developing country. However formidable their resources and people, most nations depended initially on foreign money and bankers to help them finance their trade.

It is not just in the 1980s either that countries have been unable or unwilling to keep up repayments to their creditors. In the Middle Ages Italian bankers were tempted by the prospect of big profits to make loans to England. To these bankers, England was a wild, developing country and a high risk because of its tribal wars, tyrannical rulers and corruption. King Edward I needed money to finance his wars and borrowed large sums from the Florentine bankers Bardi and Peruzzi. However, forty years later Edward III decided he could get his own English merchants to finance the wars, and so he defaulted on the Italian debts. The Bardi and Peruzzi banks collapsed.

Loans have helped many countries, including the United States, Russia and Japan, to increase their output and trade and to become economically independent. As late as the nineteenth century, the United States still depended on London investors and bankers to finance its development. Money flowed into state bonds. But the governments of the individual states did not want to raise taxes to repay the interest. When they hit economic problems in the early 1840s the states of Maryland and

Right: *Edward III of England (1312–77) was one of the first leaders to default on the repayment of national debts.*

15

Pennsylvania announced that they were defaulting on their repayments. Other states, including Mississippi and Louisiana, followed suit. The banks were criticized for encouraging poor states to take on loans they could not afford to repay. Over time most of the states reached agreements with their creditors to resume payment on the old loans and to contract further loans. But one state, Mississippi, has never repaid its debts.

After World War II Europe was in urgent need of finance for reconstruction. The continent was in a very bad way; it had been torn apart by war and its economy was disintegrating. In 1947 the U.S. Secretary of State, General Marshall, came up with a proposal for generous amounts of aid to Europe, provided that the program of reconstruction was organized by the European countries themselves. The Marshall Plan led, over the next few years, to the American Congress approving funds of $13 billion – an amount that would be worth at least ten times as much today.

This money was *given*, not lent! At this point in history it was the United States that held the world's purse strings. It chose to help both Europe and itself by restoring Europe's economic strength and establishing markets and trading partners for American industry. No other aid program has been as generous or has changed the economic balance of the world as profoundly.

The treatment of developing countries today could hardly be more different from the generous treatment of Europe under the Marshall Plan. The world's economic scales are tipped very firmly in favor of the Western industrialized powers, as we shall see in the next section.

The docklands at Bremen, now East Germany, devastated by bombing in World War II. Almost total destruction of industrial areas seriously affected the economy of Europe.

Above: *General Marshall headed one of the most generous financial aid programs ever proposed. The money from the United States helped revive the European economy.*

Unequal shares

Almost all the developing countries staggering under the burden of debt today have at some stage been colonies of the European powers. Colonialism dramatically changed their economies. They became the providers of cheap raw materials for European industries and the buyers of manufactured goods – often made from the very same materials but costing very much more – from Europe. This system helped make Europe rich while it left the colonies poor. Many people had land on which they grew their food taken from them. Large plantations were established to grow crops specifically for export.

Colonialism set a pattern of production and trade that has largely continued into modern times. The recent famine in Africa was not caused simply by drought. Africa has more than enough food to feed itself, but even while millions of people were dying of starvation, huge quantities of food were being exported to the rich countries of the world.

Below: *Cotton is produced in Ethiopia for sale to other nations. It brings in foreign currency in return but does not help feed the people suffering from drought.*

Although the Spanish and Portuguese colonies in Central and South America gained their independence a century and a half ago, they too have borne the lasting imprint of colonialism. The indigenous Indian peoples who were forced off the fertile land still live in poverty. The recent rapid growth of industries in Latin America, which loans from the West have helped to finance, has been of little benefit to the poor people.

The poorest countries, mostly in Africa and Asia, and the countries of Latin America that have increased their industrial output are all subject to the greater economic power of the richer Western nations. The Western countries have the real influence over world trade and finance.

When developing countries began building factories and exporting their own manufactured goods Western countries imposed tariffs on imported goods. They also set up quotas that limited the amount of goods that could be imported. Although a General Agreement on Tariffs and Trade (GATT) was established in 1948 by Western nations to lower tariffs among themselves, it was not applied to imports from developing countries. In 1976, a new institution, the United Nations Conference on Trade and Development (UNCTAD), was set up to try to work out a fairer deal. It has called for real reforms that would benefit developing countries, but Western nations have mainly resisted these changes.

World recession has made the situation even more unfairly weighted against the developing countries. Manufactured goods have become more expensive while prices of raw materials have fallen. So developing countries have to export more than ever before just to pay for the same amount of imports and for the interest on their debts. It is like having to run extra fast just to stay on the spot.

> Alice looked round her in great surprise. "Why, I do believe we've been under this tree all the time. Everything is just as it was!"
> "Of course it is," said the Queen. "What would you have it?"
> "Well, in our country," said Alice, still panting a little, "you'd generally get to somewhere else – if you ran very fast for a long time, as we've been doing."
> "A slow sort of country!" said the Queen. "Now, here, you see, it takes all the running *you* can do, to keep in the same place. If you want to get somewhere else, you must run at least twice as fast as that!"
> *from Through the Looking-Glass by Lewis Carroll*

Copper smelting furnaces in Chile. The price of copper has been falling since the mid-1970s, at the same time oil prices have risen.

Korem refugee camp in Ethiopia where hundreds of thousands of people have received food and medical supplies. Emergency aid from overseas helps save lives, but does not solve the problem of famine in Africa.

Controlling the world's financial system

Two institutions were set up in 1944 to prevent the world's finances from getting completely out of control as they had done during the Great Crash and Great Depression. These were the International Monetary Fund (IMF) and the International Bank for Reconstruction and Development, now generally known as the World Bank.

The original purpose of the IMF was to provide short-term loans to industrialized countries recovering from World War II, but in practice most of the loans have been to developing countries. The IMF will lend only to countries that agree to its conditions. These conditions consist of a number of measures to increase the money earned on exports and cut back public spending, which includes money spent on hospitals and schools. This makes life even harder for poor people in the debtor countries. Since the loans are intended to be paid back over a short period, they are of little help in long-term development that could help the prosperity of the country.

The World Bank lends money to member countries for development projects such as building roads, dams, power plants and other projects to improve infrastructure and industry. Because such plans often require input from foreign industry and experts, the Western industrialized nations also benefit from the funding.

Both the World Bank and the IMF are largely controlled by the Western countries, who make the largest contribution to these funds. The developing countries, who also make contributions but much smaller ones, have comparatively little influence over the way the organizations are run and the conditions they impose on the debtor nations.

Affiliated to the World Bank, the International Development Administration (IDA) was set up in 1960 to provide long-term loans at low interest rates to the poorest member countries. If the IDA is to be of any real assistance to these countries its funds need to be regularly replenished, something that some Western nations – particularly the United States – have often been reluctant to do.

3 Whose crisis?

When we talk about the debt crisis, who do we think of as being affected by the problems?

When the debt crisis broke in 1982, and in the months that followed Mexico's announcement that it was suspending repayments, country after country had to renegotiate the terms of its debts. There was controlled panic among bankers and governments of industrialized countries. The threat was not just to individual banks but also to the financial system as a whole. Banks do much business among themselves, lending to and borrowing from each other. In the 1970s, in order to spread the risks of lending, they had joined together in syndicates to make loans. The fear was that any bank threatened with bad debts would in turn bring those from which it had borrowed into danger. Public confidence would fall away, depositors would withdraw their money and a domino reaction would eventually lead to the collapse of the entire financial system.

In the late 1980s, the word *default* no longer inspires the same fear and panic among bankers. They have learned to live with the crisis, to adjust to it, to take precautionary measures against possible non-payment of part of the debts. Although the loans to developing countries no longer yield huge profits, in the first half of the 1980s they provided substantial returns, as the graph shows. The leading American bank, Citicorp, made 20 percent of its entire profits from Brazil alone.

But the crisis has taken its toll on Western countries. Developing countries have been squeezed by debt problems, and the IMF has imposed policies designed to make them less dependent on imports so that they have money with which to pay the interest on their debts. Because of this, Western countries have lost important markets for their exports. This has been a major cause of unemployment in the West.

The greatest burden has fallen, though, on the debtor countries themselves and above all on the poorest people in these countries. They

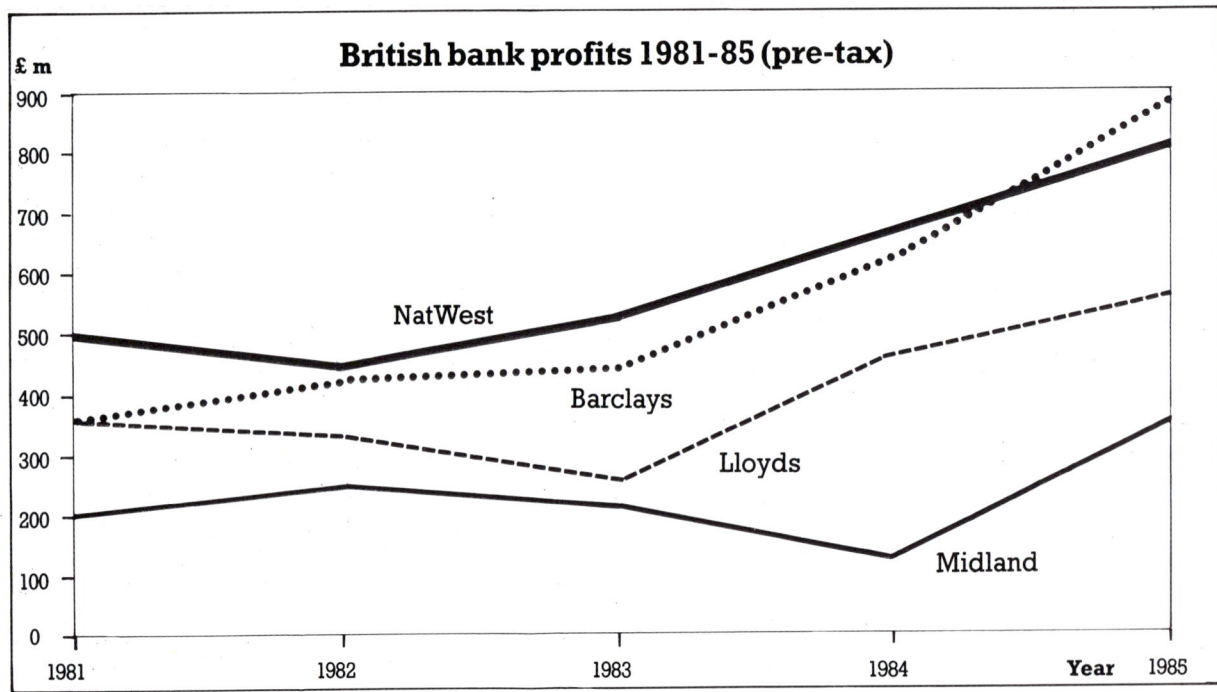

are the ones who experience the crisis in their daily struggle for survival.

The burden on the poor

Children in Brazil selling goods on the street. Poor families have to find ways of surviving when there is no income from secure jobs.

> – The number of severely hungry and malnourished children in Africa has risen by 25 percent in the last decade.
> – In Chile and Ghana elementary-school attendance has been falling and drop-out rates increasing.
> – In Latin America there are many millions of children living on the streets.
> – Between 1979 and 1983 expenditure per head on health decreased in 60 percent of Latin American countries.
> – In Jamaica charges have been introduced for services that were previously free, while patients in hospitals have to bring their own linen and food to survive.
> *from Adjustment with a Human Face, Unicef report 1987*

During the great lending spree of the 1970s there is little evidence that the poor people, who are the majority in developing countries, benefited greatly from the loans. In many countries the rich and powerful became richer and more powerful. This, of course, depended a great deal on the kinds of development strategies adopted by particular countries. Some countries, such as Tanzania, have tried to limit the scale of private business and to prevent large foreign companies from moving in and taking over much of the economy. They have encouraged people to stand on their own feet and have organized community development in rural areas. Brazil, on the other hand, has pursued a policy of growth above everything. It has developed very fast but in a very lop-sided way. There is a huge gap between the rich and the poor. In 1985 it was revealed, for example, that 45 percent of the land was owned by just 1 percent of the population. The small wealthy sector of Venezuela's population also benefited greatly from the loans at the expense of the poor. Enormous sums of money in fact left the country to be invested in bank accounts in the West.

After 1982 the flow of finance from the West to the developing countries was drastically cut back. By 1985 poor countries were actually paying out *more* to rich countries than they received from them. The traditional direction for the overall flow of money – from the developed to the developing world – had been reversed. The IMF's prescribed "medicine" has been for countries to adjust their economies to the new circumstances. An adjustment program has a number of basic ingredients: exporting more and importing less in order to earn the foreign exchange to meet payments on debts; reducing government spending on public services such as health and education; keeping wages down; removing subsidies that keep down the price of basic foods. It is obvious that such measures are bound to hit the poor hardest of all. We will now look in closer detail at how the debt crisis has affected particular countries.

Brazil started getting into difficulties in the early 1980s. It implemented an adjustment program that led to the currency's being devalued several times. Devaluation means bringing down the value of a currency as compared with other currencies. The purpose is to encourage foreign buyers to buy a country's goods since devaluation effectively lowers the price of these goods. But devaluation also raises the prices of imports, many of which are essential goods needed by ordinary people. Public spending on essential services was cut and wage increases were held back. Between 1981 and 1983, 1.8 million more people started working in the "informal sector" because they had lost their jobs or because there were no

The contrast between the rich people and the poor people of Brazil is clear in Rio de Janeiro where the shanty town borders on the more affluent high-rise housing.

Many children and women in Brazil do heavy work such as in this brick factory.

openings and no security of employment for them in the regular job market.

To reduce imports of oil, Brazil concentrated on making sugarcane alcohol as a substitute for gasoline, a policy that also had adverse effects on the poor. Food production decreased sharply as great tracts of land were taken over and used to grow sugar and export crops. This in turn had an impact on health. In São Paolo State the effects of a measles epidemic in 1984 were magnified because so many children were undernourished. Infant mortality rates rose for Brazil as a whole and the number of emergency consultations in hospitals grew. As spending on education was reduced, the school system deteriorated badly too. A serious result of the crisis has been that a growing number of children have been abandoned by their parents, particularly in urban areas, and more children have turned to crime.

In June 1987 the Brazilian government introduced further drastic adjustment measures to try to control inflation. Cutting the subsidy on wheat caused the price of bread to go up by 36 percent, while prices of public transportation, the telephone service and electricity all rose sharply too. Rioters set buses on fire in Rio de Janeiro in protest at the 50 percent rise in state bus fares, and on another occasion there was a stone-throwing attack on a bus that was carrying the President.

Jamaica is ranked as a middle-income country by the World Bank. But the country's wealth is possessed by a very small section of the population while the majority of the people live in poverty. By the end of the 1970s Jamaica was hopelessly in debt and was forced to turn to the IMF for assistance. Michael Manley's government reached an agreement with the IMF, but the harsh conditions involved made the cost of living soar while wages remained low. The government tried in vain to persuade the IMF to modify its conditions and was defeated in the general election of 1980 largely because of the bitterly unpopular economic program. The new government, under Edward Seaga, found more favor with the IMF, which did not, at first, impose such tough conditions as before. However, in 1982 a crisis in the bauxite industry – on which Jamaica depended for two-thirds of its export earnings – coincided with a sharp rise in interest rates, which made the foreign debt more expensive to repay. In 1983 the government began devaluing the Jamaican dollar.

Rising prices caused great suffering among the poor. By 1984 it was estimated that a five-person household spending 75 percent of its income on food would be able to buy only half of what it needed to maintain a healthy diet. Between 1983 and 1985 the cost of electricity tripled. Cuts in government spending affected essential services. Spending on health went down by 33 percent between 1981 and 1985, affecting the supply of drugs and equipment and leading to a shortage of trained personnel. When charges were introduced into the health service the poorest people were unable to afford medical treatment. Spending on education was reduced by 40 percent. The result has been badly maintained school buildings, staff shortages, overcrowding and poor standards. Many children do not go to school at all. As the prices of books, clothing and public transportation increase, more and more parents are having to keep their children at home.

National nutrition surveys show increasing malnutrition among children, particularly those in the urban areas where it is not possible for people to supplement their diet by growing their own food. The number of children suffering from malnutrition who were admitted to the island's major children's hospital more than doubled between 1978 and 1985.

Many Jamaicans live in very basic housing with no running water or electricity.

A Zambian woman doing her washing. The poorest people in Zambia suffered most from the effects of IMF "economic reforms."

> "Must we starve our children to pay our debts?"
> *Julius Nyerere, former president of Tanzania*

Many of the poorest countries in the world are to be found on the African continent, and these countries are now further crippled by debt. Although the volume of debt cannot be compared to that of Latin America (the continent's debt is about the same size as Brazil's) for the very poor African economies the debt weighs heavily.

Zambia is one of twenty-seven African countries to have accepted adjustment programs from the IMF. It kept strictly to the agreed terms for four years, but by May 1987 the strain had become so great that it decided to break off the agreement. The country has been beset by economic difficulties in recent years. It depends on copper for 90 percent of its export earnings, but the world price of copper fell by 60 percent between 1974 and 1984. There have been frequent periods of drought, and transportation problems caused by wars in neighboring Angola and Mozambique. The IMF package involved a number of economic "reforms" that reduced incomes and employment, abolished subsidies, which resulted in higher food prices, and cut back essential services.

In December 1986 the price of corn meal was raised again, this time by 120 percent. Food riots broke out in the country's copperbelt, claiming fifteen lives. These were followed by strikes by teachers, nurses and postmen, whose wages had been kept at unacceptably low levels. Faced with ever-growing discontent, President Kaunda abandoned the IMF's economic program. In a late-night broadcast to the nation he announced that the deal was over, that price controls would be reintroduced and severe limits would be imposed on debt-service payments. But Zambia still owes $5.8 billion, and unless it receives new loans on easier terms, it is likely to get into even greater difficulties.

The Philippines is the fifth largest debtor nation, after Brazil, Mexico, Argentina and Venezuela. Much of the debt was incurred during the corrupt Marcos regime, and many Filipinos argue that it is unfair that the poor should have to pay for the corruption and mismanagement of former rulers. As a result of adjustment programs since 1983 the unemployment rate has risen and earnings have fallen. This has happened in a country that was already highly unequal in its distribution of wealth. Much of the poverty is found in the rural areas, among farmers, laborers and small fishermen. The urban poor live mainly in Manila, working in the "informal sector." As real wages have gone down and unemployment worsened, more households have fallen below the poverty line. Malnutrition in children under five went up 5 percent between 1982 and 1985. The fall in infant mortality rates slowed down, and there was a sharp rise in infant mortality among the black population. As poverty increased, so also did the number of street children trying to scratch a living from begging or stealing.

> Official: "You'll just have to tighten your belt."
> Citizen: "I can't. I ate it yesterday."
> *Joke from Peru*

Guerrilla fighters in the Philippines. The New People's Army opposed the corrupt, debt-ridden regime of ex-President Marcos, and remains a problem for the current government headed by President Corazon Aquino.

African women farmers are traditionally responsible for tasks such as weeding, planting and harvesting.

Women pay

> "We're always asking ourselves, we housewives, what did we do that we have to pay this foreign debt? Have our children eaten too well or gone to the best schools? Worn the best clothes? Or have our salaries been too high? Have we better houses? We all shout in unison, No! ... So who has benefited? Why are we the ones who have to pay the debt?"

Women in developing countries have paid a very high price for the debts run up by their governments. In particular, IMF austerity policies, designed to put the economy in order and to deal with balance of payment problems, can have a devastating effect on women.

Cuts in government spending involve, for a start, the removal of food subsidies. Since women are traditionally responsible for looking after the needs of the family, they are the ones who have to try to make up for the rise in food prices. Very often this means that they eat less themselves so that the men and other members of the family have enough. Health services are also hit by government cuts, and this affects women in many different ways. Women use health services more than men and suffer most when services are reduced. The majority of lower paid workers in the health services throughout the world are women, and cuts mean that many of them lose their jobs. When fees for medical treatment are introduced, the number of women attending ante-natal clinics drops considerably. This happened in Jamaica in 1984 and was accompanied by a sharp rise in the number of women dying in childbirth. As basic food items go up in price and health services decline, more mothers and children suffer from malnutrition, and the birth weight of babies goes down.

Women's education suffers from the economic crisis too. Girls are more likely than boys to be kept away from school when families cannot afford higher bus fares or more expensive school books. In communities where adult literacy or women's education classes are run, progress is hindered by poor health and the heavy burden of women's work.

In many countries, particularly in Africa, the debt crisis has meant an even greater emphasis on the production of cash crops in order to earn more from exports. Women are the traditional farmers in Africa, responsible for over 70 percent of all agricultural work, and food crops for local consumption are nearly always grown by women. Yet cash-crop farming – growing food to sell rather than to eat – has mainly been introduced to men, and women's role in agricultural development and in providing for their families has been largely ignored. As more and more land is taken over for cash crops, women have to try to find alternative ways of feeding their families. Often they are required to assist with cash-crop farming too, carrying out the back-breaking tasks of planting and weeding in addition to the rest of their heavy work load: fetching water and firewood, cooking and looking after the children.

A tea-picker in Kenya. Many women have to assist with cash-crop farming and so have less time to spend on growing food for their families.

The industrializing countries of Asia and Latin America have also geared their production to export. In some cases this has meant that the women have been left behind in the rural areas to fend for themselves and their families while their menfolk have gone in search of work in the factories and mines. In other cases, companies have recruited women because they can pay them less than men for the unskilled, repetitive and often extremely tiring jobs on the assembly lines of new industries such as electronics. These women can be as young as sixteen years of age or less. They usually live in hostels, away from their families, and work long hours for low wages under appalling conditions. After a few years of peering into a microscope their eyesight can be ruined.

> "The manual dexterity of the oriental female is famous the world over. Her hands are small and she works fast and with extreme care. Who could be better qualified by nature and inheritance to contribute to the efficiency of a bench-assembly production line than an oriental girl?"
> *Malaysian government investment brochure*

This practice has so far taken place mainly in Asia, which is often held up as an example to the rest of the developing world of how to manage economic affairs successfully. But women have paid dearly for this "success."

The threat to peace

It is obvious that the effects of debt and economic crisis do not help a country's stability. The harsh conditions they create have caused mass demonstrations, strikes and riots in many developing countries, sometimes involving serious injury or loss of life – as in the case of the riots in Zambia in December 1986. In Latin America the debts of many countries were incurred under military dictatorships in the 1970s. Most of these countries have now returned to civilian rule but the new, more democratic, governments start off at a great disadvantage as they bear the enormous burden of having to manage their countries' debts. The unpopularity of most of the measures so far adopted to deal with the crisis threatens the survival of these governments and increases the danger of further military coups.

Many women in the Far East work in factories producing electronic equipment. Although the work looks physically undemanding, it can have harmful effects on workers' eyesight.

History has shown how dangerous an economic crisis can be. After World War I Germany was required to pay excessive amounts of money as reparation for its part in the war. This put an intolerable strain on an already bankrupt economy. The Great Depression that followed the Wall Street Crash of 1929 made Europe weak and vulnerable, and this sequence of economic crises is seen as a major cause of the rise of Fascism and Nazism in the years preceding World War II. It is not difficult to draw a comparison between German reparations and the excessive debt payment that developing countries are forced to make today. Furthermore, if there were a series of defaults and the global economic system really did collapse, the threat to world peace would be enormous.

The debt to the environment

The destruction of the environment, which is taking place at an alarming rate and in turn exacts a huge social and human toll, cannot be separated from the economic policies of recent decades. Every year almost 15 million acres of productive land are turned into worthless desert, while vast areas of the world are being stripped of their forests. The air and the sea are being polluted, lakes are dying, fertile top soil is being eroded. In short, the ecological balance of the world is under severe threat.

Huge areas of agricultural land in the Sudan are used for cash-crop production. This sugarcane estate probably replaced dozens of smallholdings, forcing the original farmers to move away.

The environment has been ruthlessly exploited for whatever can make money.

The production of cash crops is just one example of this tendency. It is often controlled by huge transnational corporations and is frequently undertaken without consideration of the consequences for the environment. In the Sudan, for example, over-production of wheat has exhausted the land in many areas and turned it into a dust bowl. When the best, most fertile land is taken over for cash-crop production this also has the effect of pushing subsistence farmers onto the poorer land. In the Sahel area of Africa – the sparse grassland area south of the Sahara Desert – more and more of this marginal land is being cultivated year after year, the amount of food it yields is steadily falling and the land is slowly being turned into desert.

As the pressure to earn enough foreign currency to keep up with debt payments increases, so also does the tendency to exploit the land excessively.

Right: *The poor people of the Sudan are left to farm the most arid and infertile soil.*

4 Debt management

The creditors' "solutions"

> "Those who wield power, control money."
> *Arusha Initiative, 1980*

Since the international debt crisis broke in August 1982, the panic that traveled through banking circles has subsided and the global financial system has not collapsed. But the crisis is not yet over. For millions of people in the debt-ridden countries it is experienced in terms of the worsening conditions of their daily lives. The truth is that so far the debt crisis has been controlled, not solved. The global debt actually grew from $825 billion in 1982 to over $1,000 billion in 1987.

In this chapter we will look at some of the approaches to the problem of debt that have been adopted so far by bankers, international institutions and governments. We begin with the creditors, because they are the ones who have been in the best position to call the tune.

The classic remedy used by creditors has been rescheduling. This means renegotiating loans so that they are paid back in smaller amounts over a longer period. The purpose is quite simply to try to prevent the debtor countries from defaulting. Both the commercial banks and Western governments have been involved in this process. After Mexico's moratorium in 1982, countries lined up to reschedule their debts and many have been forced to arrange several reschedulings. But the effect of repeated reschedulings has been to increase the debt burden, not to reduce it.

Most reschedulings have been agreed under conditions imposed by the International Monetary Fund. The countries that had run up large debts with the commercial banks were the first to be dealt with when the crisis broke. The IMF lent these countries money and also persuaded the banks to make additional loans so the countries could keep up interest payments.

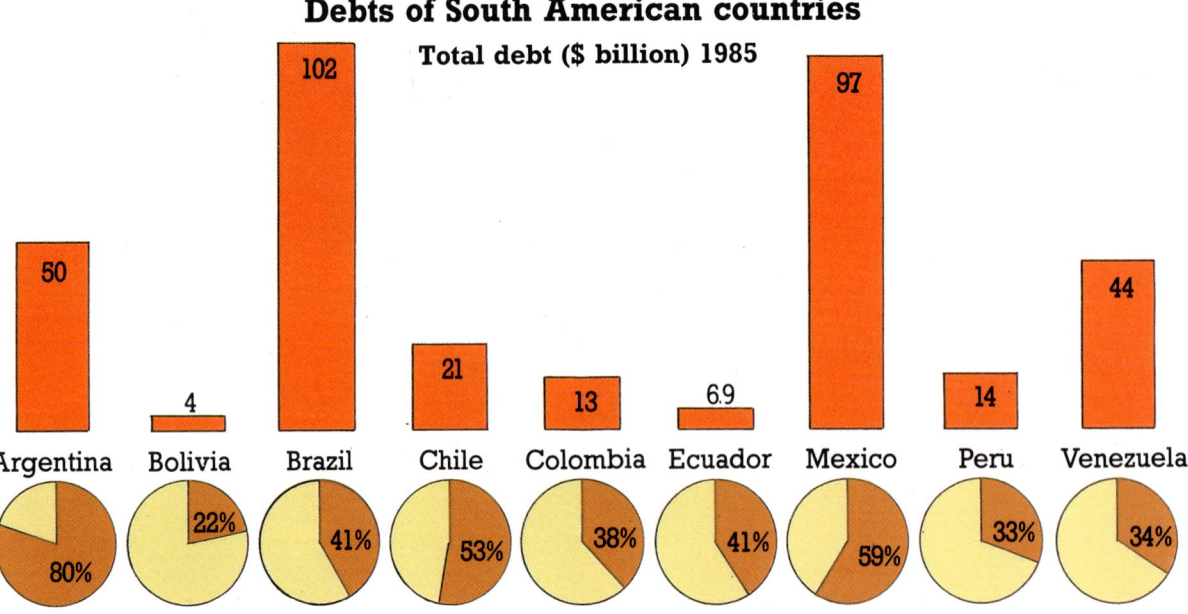

Debts of South American countries
Total debt ($ billion) 1985

Debt payment as % of exports

32

The banks had very little choice about agreeing to this kind of arrangement – they made the loans reluctantly and very cautiously – but the loans they made were very much smaller than before. Meanwhile, the banks gradually reduced the amount of business they did with developing countries.

The poorer countries that had not been considered creditworthy by the banks during the great lending spree of the 1970s were mainly in debt to Western governments, who also insisted in almost every case that a debtor country agree to an IMF adjustment program before its debts could be rescheduled. This process has now continued for several years.

The busy dealing room of a European bank. Although banks are still lending money to developing countries (and still have huge loans outstanding), they are more reluctant to do so than they were ten years ago.

Whenever a debtor country asks for a longer period to pay its debts, the "Club of Paris" meets to work out an agreement. The Club is an informal grouping of the Western countries, whose membership varies depending on who the main creditors are. The Club exists to see that debtor countries honor their repayment commitments; it has no interest in supporting development efforts.

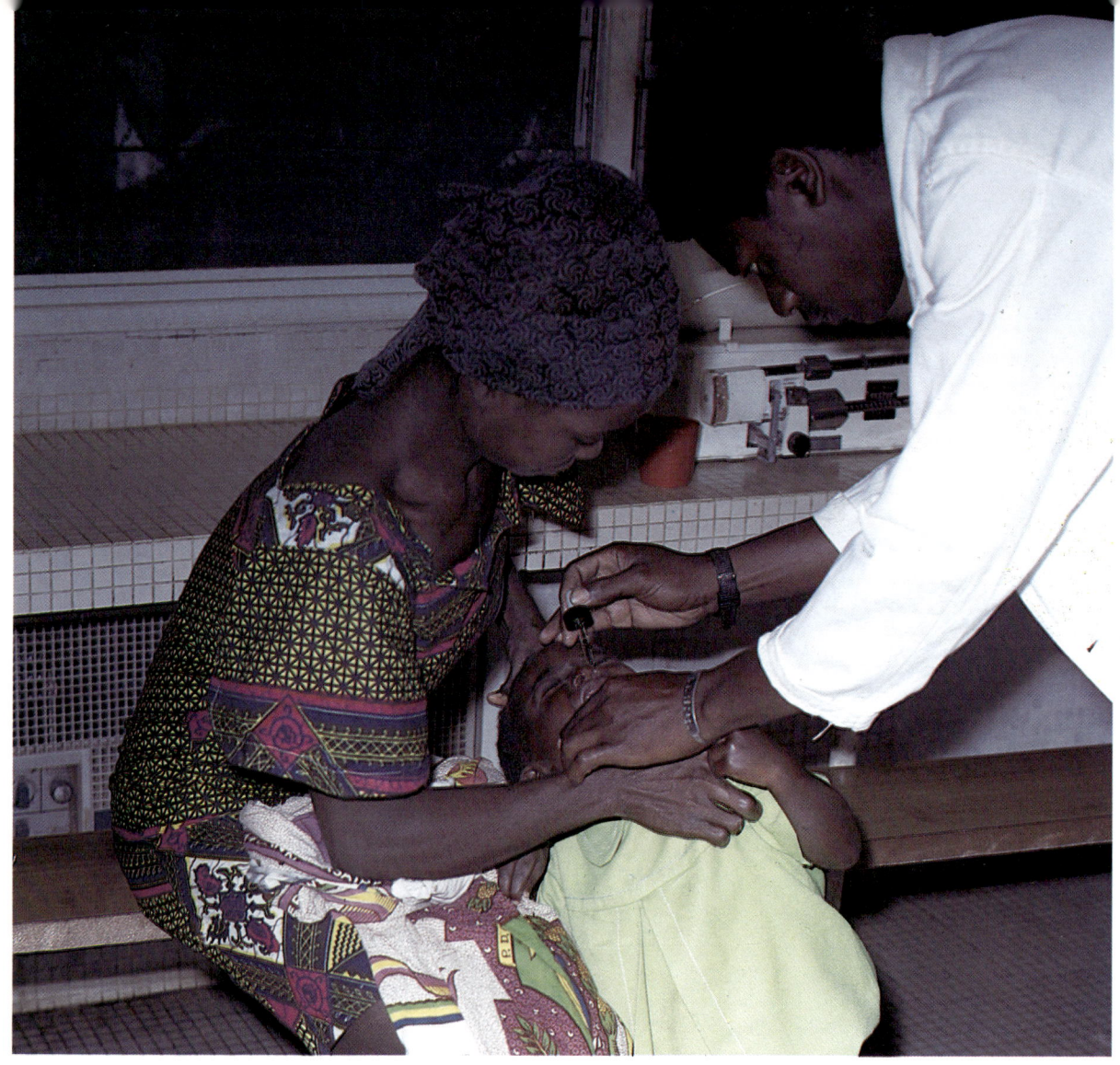

We have already seen that IMF conditions may cause severe problems for developing countries since they may require governments to make cuts in social services and employment. Nor do such adjustment programs necessarily mean economic growth. For adjustment to succeed, investment must be kept up. Without adequate investment the result of adjustment may be recession rather than recovery.

The normal practice with rescheduling has been to arrange that loans falling due over a period of one or two years are repaid instead over five to eight years. But this is simply not enough time for debtor countries to get back on their feet. Many people think that repayment periods of fifty years or more are needed for the countries with the heaviest debt burdens.

Vaccination programs are very important for the general health of a country, but they are the kind of service that may be hit by the IMF's adjustment measures.

The Baker Plan

After 1982 there were three years during which Latin America experienced a recession worse than in the 1930s. In Africa the average income dropped to below the level of the 1970s. It became clear that something was wrong with the strategy of short-term rescheduling combined with the kind of contraction of the economy required by the IMF. Besides, the IMF was beginning to accumulate arrears as debtor countries fell behind with repayments.

In October 1985 the Treasury Secretary of the United States, James Baker, put forward a new plan that marked a political shift in the way debt problems were handled. There were various elements to the plan. One was to take steps to deal with some of the problems caused by Western nations, including getting them to agree to reduce the value of the U.S. dollar, which would also reduce the value of the debts as most of them were held in dollars. A year later the value of the US dollar had dropped by 22 percent. Other measures, however, like dealing with protectionism, had not been achieved. The central part of the plan was to encourage economic growth in the fifteen largest debtor countries. Baker proposed that the banks, Western governments and the World Bank come up with an extra $30 billion of loans to these countries.

The trouble was that, first, the sum of money proposed was still totally inadequate to deal with the huge scale of the problem, and second, it still depended on debtor countries taking the kind of adjustment measures that were so unpopular with the ordinary citizens of the countries. Although the banks released some new money, the amount fell far short even of the figure Baker had proposed.

The fact remains that debtor countries are still paying out more in debt repayments than the finance they are receiving. The flow of money is still going in the wrong direction.

A Japanese plan to help ease the debt

The Tokyo stock exchange at work. The Japanese economy is so successful that it is possible for the government to give substantial financial assistance to developing countries.

problem was devised in 1987. The plan was to channel, over a period of three years, $30 billion of Japanese money into developing countries through the World Bank. The debtor countries most likely to benefit from the program were the Baker Plan countries. The program was dubbed by some people as the "Japanese Marshall Plan," although the proposed finance fell a long way short of that. All the same, it looked like an important step forward.

One of the curious things about the debt crisis is that there is now a flourishing market in debt. Increasingly, banks have been selling off part of their debt (although only a small proportion of the total) to transnational companies. The debt is sold at a discount – at, for example, 80 percent or 60 percent or even 20 percent of its original value. This process of "debt-equity swaps" results in foreign companies having a bigger stake in the economy of developing countries. It certainly does not help the poor, who go on being impoverished.

The debtors' strategies

Between 1982 and 1984 creditor governments and banks, with powerful IMF support, took the lead in controlling the debt crisis. The gains they achieved were very much at the expense of the developing countries. But as social unrest has grown in response to rising unemployment, higher food prices and shrinking social services, the governments of debtor countries have tried to find their own ways of dealing with the crisis. In theory, debtor nations hold the trump card; they are the ones who owe the money and they could simply refuse to pay their debts. In practice, of course, it is not as easy as that. But the question remains whether major debtor nations can use debtor power to bargain with, and get a better deal from, the West. Latin American countries have adopted a variety of approaches so far.

In June 1984 there was a meeting in Cartagena, Colombia, of representatives of eleven debtor governments: Argentina, Bolivia, Brazil, Chile, Colombia, Ecuador, Mexico, Peru, Uruguay, Venezuela and the Dominican Republic. They called for strong measures to deal with the crisis. These included reducing interest rates, limiting the amount of money earned from exports that could be spent on debt repayments, and extending the periods over which they had to repay their loans. However, although the group has met several times and repeated their demands, they have not succeeded in taking any collective action that would really put pressure on the West. One major obstacle is that the debt giants like Mexico and Brazil are in a better position to make more favorable individual agreements with their creditors. But, by the same token, they are also in a strong position to take initiatives that would help the poorer countries. For a long time this did not happen. With its moratorium in February 1987, however, Brazil took a lead that should help other countries drive harder bargains with foreign bankers.

The first Latin American country to take radical action to deal with its economic crisis was Peru. In August 1985 President Alan Garcia, whose party had been elected to government by a sizable majority four months before, announced that Peru would use no more than 10 percent of its export earnings to repay its long-term debts. The idea was to use the rest

Dr. Alan Garcia during the Peruvian election campaign of 1985. Soon after becoming President he took action to limit debt repayments.

of the money it got from overseas trade to help expand production, which would then enable the country to increase the amount it paid to its creditors. But if trade was reduced in value for any reason – such as a fall in commodity prices on the world market – debt repayments would be reduced too. Peru also gave preference in its debt servicing to the international institutions like the World Bank; the commer-

One of the measures taken by President Garica of Peru to try to increase his government's control of the economy was to nationalize the banks in September 1987. This meant that all the bank signs had to be changed.

cial banks were put at the bottom of the list of priorities. The IMF then refused the country any more loans and Peru promptly responded

Although Cuba does not have large debts to Western banks or governments, its leader, Fidel Castro, has strong views on the action debtor countries should take to protect themselves against huge interest charges.

by suspending its repayments to the IMF.

Peru's lead was followed by Nigeria, which for a brief time limited its repayments to 30 percent of export earnings. Others, like Bolivia, in 1984, and Ecuador, in 1987, have refused to pay altogether.

The Cuban leader, Fidel Castro, goes further still (although Cuba itself does not have large debts) and advocates a "can't pay, won't pay" approach. He argues that debt service obligations need to be suspended for at least ten to twenty years. "My opinion is that no other alternative exists. To try to collect this debt, at least in Latin America, would be socially explosive."

5 The need for change

"Money is like muck, not good except it be spread."
Francis Bacon, sixteenth-century social commentator

The problem of debt in developing countries is extremely complex and there are, of course, no easy ways of solving it. But so far the approach to the problem has been to muddle through and make arrangements on a country-by-country basis, when clearly what is needed is firm and far-reaching action. The West has, on the whole, taken the line that the crisis is containable and that only a minimum amount of action by governments and banks is necessary to ensure that debt servicing continues. But the cracks in the system are becoming increasingly visible.

Events in 1987, for example, were a dramatic reminder that the crisis had not gone away. In February there was the announcement of a moratorium on debt payments by Brazil, the developing world's largest debtor. *The Observer* newspaper described the action like this:

> With the momentous move on repayments, Brazil is bidding to take the world's debt crisis out of the hands of the bankers and put it firmly where the debtors have long thought it belongs: in the laps of the world's governments.

Street beggars in Brazil. More needs to be done to help the poorest people of society, but until the problem of debt is solved, this is unlikely to happen.

Then came a great increase in bad debt provisions by the international banks: sums set aside by the banks against money they do not believe they will get back. In May the largest American bank, Citicorp, announced it was increasing its provisions from $2 billion to $5 billion. This move was followed by similar action by major British banks, although on a smaller scale. So the banks are taking realistic measures to protect themselves, but this does not mean they have canceled any debts. They are still officially saying that they expect payment in full, but by making these provisions they can declare lower profits and therefore pay considerably less tax.

If the debt problem does indeed belong "in the laps of the world's governments", what steps can they take toward solving the crisis? There have been many suggestions of positive action that could be taken, despite the complexities of the situation. We will look finally at some of the possibilities for dealing more effectively with debt and for finding a fairer way forward.

Increasing the flow of finance to developing countries

The present situation, where more resources flow from developing countries to the richer nations than the other way around, must be brought to an end. For this to happen there needs to be a substantial increase in the flow of finance from the developed countries. Two British economists, Harold Lever and Christopher Huhne, in a report entitled *Debt and Danger*, call for a new plan in which $20–30 billion per year would be channeled to the debtor countries. They suggest that Western governments should guarantee new commercial bank lending to developing countries. Other people have pointed out that banks as commercial organizations whose purpose is

Brazil earns foreign currency in a number of ways, including producing Volkswagen vans. But 41 percent of the money coming into the country goes out again in debt repayments.

to make maximum profits are unsuited to providing the large amounts of money needed. No real solution will be found until direct government lending, or lending via the international institutions, is increased. Part of the money should come from an increase in aid from developed countries. Government aid from many countries has not increased in recent years and it must be stepped up again.

Reducing debt payments

Action should be taken to bring down interest rates. Because the United States has not had sufficient income to cover expenditure and has not raised enough in taxes, it has tried to narrow the gap by keeping interest rates high to encourage foreign investment. If the United

In a shanty town outside Lima, Peru, people wait in line to collect water in buckets. President Garcia is trying in a number of ways to improve the economy in order to bring new prosperity to the nation. But will he succeed?

States government kept tighter control over its budget deficit, interest rates could be lowered. Governments could also agree to subsidize interest rates for developing countries, or banks could agree to reduce interest rates on existing loans. War on Want in Britain has spearheaded a campaign for banks to recognize their share of responsibility for the crisis and take a cut in their profits. But this is unlikely to happen unless governments are committed to taking action. What is needed is political determination.

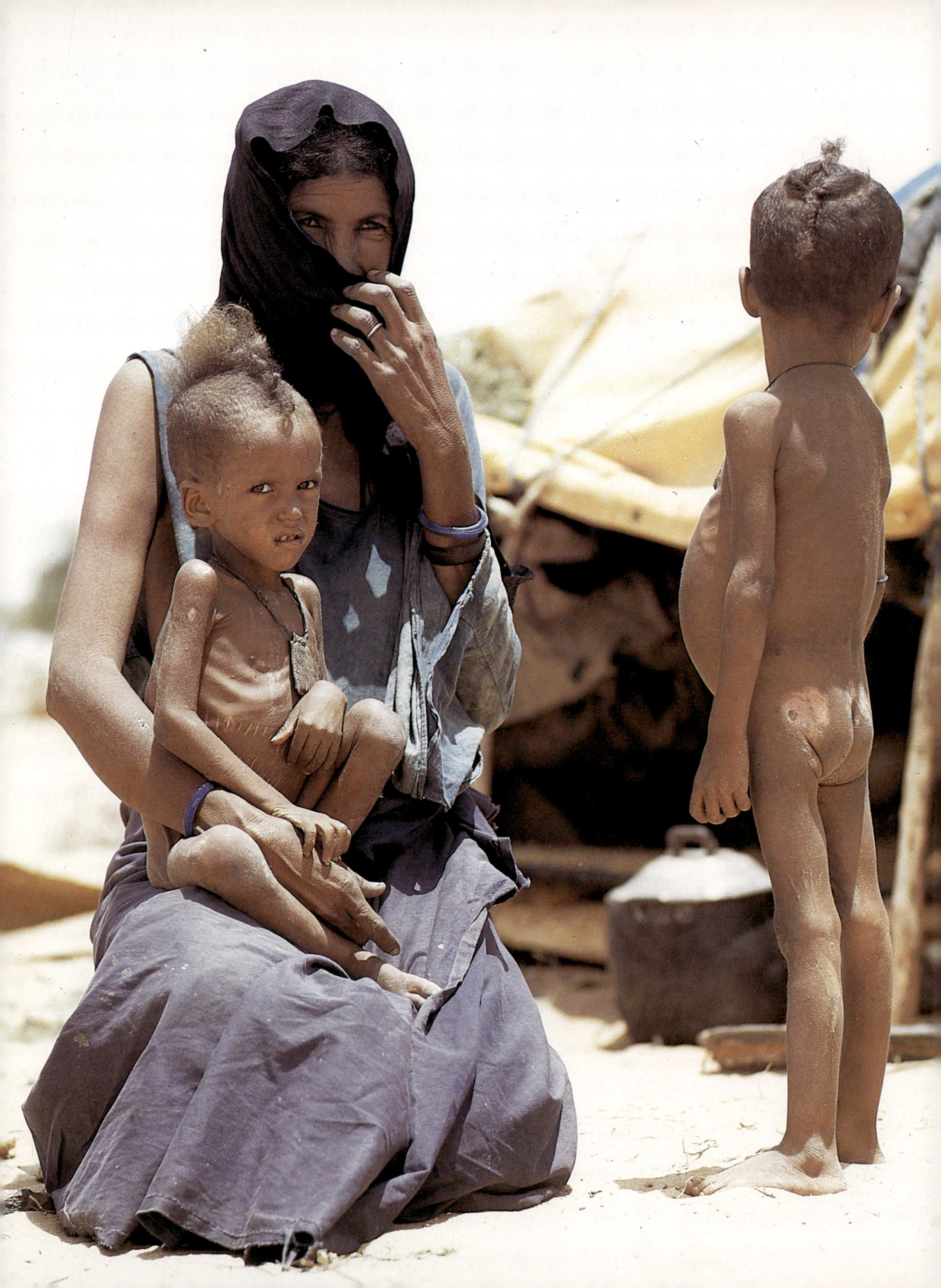

Special help for the poorest countries

The least developed countries, many of which are in sub-Saharan Africa, have such fragile economies that special measures need to be taken to help them. These could include writing off government-to-government debts and allowing much longer rescheduling periods. The British Chancellor of the Exchequer, Nigel Lawson, has been trying to push for greater debt relief for sub-Saharan Africa, but has not met with a sympathetic response, particularly from the United States and Japanese governments. However, the Club of Paris made an important concession in relaxing its rule limiting rescheduling to ten-year periods, and in June 1987 Mozambique won the most favorable rescheduling terms ever granted to a developing nation: a period of twenty years. Britain has a good record in terms of converting loans to the poorest nations into grants, but other major powers – particularly the United States and the Soviet Union – have taken very few steps to fulfil the international agreement to write off the government-to-government loans of the thirty-six least developed countries.

New money is desperately needed too. Many African countries, admitting their share in the mismanagement of their economies in the past, have introduced programs of economic reform, but without the practical support of new funds these are most likely to go on squeezing the poor.

Adjustment with a human face

Economic adjustment has had harmful effects on the poorest, most vulnerable people. Children and women from poor families have been the hardest hit. Economic decline may have been halted in many cases but only at an immense human cost. As UNICEF (United Nations Children's Fund) has argued, new adjustment policies are needed to protect the vulnerable and promote development that is relevant to the needs of the poor. Instead of harsh conditions that cut social services and raise the price of food, measures are needed to encourage food production and keep food prices at a reasonable level, to protect the environment, to cut government spending in areas like defense rather than basic services, to stop capital flight and to tax the rich rather than cutting services relevant to the poor.

Left: *Until action is taken to improve global economic conditions and to reduce the burden of debt, disasters such as famine will remain a permanent threat.*

Reforming the world's economic system

> "The international debt problem is like AIDS. It requires a global solution."
> *Babacar N'Diaye,*
> *President of the African*
> *Development Bank*

Most important of all for long-term development and prosperity, there needs to be a real shake-up of the global economic system so that poor countries have more control over their resources and their development. The IMF and World Bank need to be restructured so that developing countries have a bigger say in how they are run. These institutions would then be able to play a genuinely helpful role in promoting financial stability and economic growth. Stronger and more representative international institutions could play a part in putting pressure on the richer nations, for example the United States, to adopt more constructive economic policies. When share prices in Wall Street and then in the other major stockmarkets of the world came tumbling down in October 1987 (a bigger fall than in 1929), the United States trade and budget deficits were widely held to be behind the crash. Despite this, the U.S. government was very reluctant to cut spending or raise taxes in order to reduce the deficit. Meanwhile such events threaten to plunge the world into recession, which means, of course, that developing countries would suffer most.

We have seen that debt works hand in hand with unfair trading patterns to impoverish the developing world. Action is needed to stabilize commodity prices and reduce barriers to imports from the developing world. The EEC's agricultural policy carries a lot of the blame in allowing huge surpluses, and is in urgent need of reform.

The challenge to the world is greater than ever before. For too long governments have dragged their feet, lacking the commitment and courage to take action. But failure to take action over the debt crisis and failure to reform a grossly unfair economic system, condemns thousands of millions of women, men and children to poverty. Are we really prepared to let this happen? Or will we help influence public opinion and add our voices to the call for action?

Sugar beet production in Europe has produced a surplus of sugar in the EEC, which has meant that there is less demand for the sugar produced by developing countries.

Glossary

Adjustment measures/program Action taken to change the way the economy of a country is run.
Arrears Money that remains to be paid.
Bauxite Clay from which aluminum is extracted. It is also used in industrial processes.
Billion A thousand million.
Capital flight Removal of money (capital) from a country for investment overseas.
Cash crop A crop grown for sale (usually export) rather than to provide food.
Colonialism The exercise of administrative and political control over another country.
Commodities Goods or articles that can be bought and sold.
Congress The government of the United States, consisting of the House of Representatives and the Senate.
Creditor One to whom money is owed.
Debt-capping Setting a limit on debt payments.
Debtor One who owes money.
Debt servicing Paying interest and capital repayments on a loan.
Default Failure to pay.
Deficit/surplus A country is said to have a balance of payments deficit when its income from exports and loans is less than its payments on imports and debt repayments. A balance of payments surplus is when income is greater than payments.
Devaluation Reducing the value of a currency.
EEC European Economic Community.
Environment The world around us, both natural and man-made.
Exchange rate The price at which one currency is purchased with another.
Exports Goods sold to another country.
IMF International Monetary Fund.
Imports Goods bought from another country.
Indigenous Originating or occurring naturally in a country or region.
Inflation Increase in the general level of prices.
Informal sector Small businesses organized by individuals or families, operating outside mainstream commerce or industry. Includes selling fruit, vegetables and cooked food, repairing shoes, making and selling clothes, and prostitution.
Infrastructure Communications systems such as roads and bridges.
Interest Money paid for the use of money borrowed.
Interest rate Level at which interest is paid, as a percentage of money borrowed.
Invest To put money into a bank or business in the hope that it will increase in value.
Moratorium Suspension of payments.
Protectionism The practice of protecting domestic industries from foreign competition.
Recession A decline in economic prosperity.
Rescheduling Extending the period of time over which debts are to be repaid.
Share(s) An investment that purchases a part of a company.
Subsidy Government money used to keep down the price of goods or to support industries or agriculture.
Subsistence farming A type of farming in which most of the produce is consumed by the farmer and his or her family, leaving little or nothing to be sold at market.
Tariff Tax or duty charged on imported goods.
Transnational companies Businesses that operate in many different countries.
Write off To cancel and accept as a loss for accounting purposes.

Books to read

The Economics of Underdeveloped Countries by Michael Belshaw (Lerner, 1970)
International Trade by Kenneth Smith (Lerner, 1970)
Famine in Africa by Lloyd Timberlake (Watts, 1986)

Picture acknowledgments

Bridgeman Art Library 15; British Telecom, cover; Camera Press 16, 17, (top), 26 (Tom Fawthorp), 38 (Christian Belpaire); Cephas Picture Library 12 & 44 (Mick Rock); Robert Harding Associates 24 (Joe Clarke), 25 (Robert Cundy); Hutchison Library, cover inset (Sarah Errington), 9 (Bernard Régent), 17 (bottom), 23, 27 (Lesley McIntyre), 28, 34, 35 (Michael MacIntyre), 39 (Sarah Errington), 40 (Carlos Freire), 42; Christine Osborne 29; Oxfam 19 (Bill Wise), 31 (Jeremy Hartley); Rex Features 11, 13, 36 (Julio Etchart); South American Pictures (Tony Morrison) frontispiece, 18, 21, 22, 37, 41; Topham 30 (Christine Osborne). All other pictures from the Wayland Picture Library.

© Copyright 1988 Wayland (Publishers) Ltd
61 Western Road, Hove, East Sussex
BN3 1JD England

Index

The numbers in **bold** refer to the pictures.

adjustment measures (program) 19, 22, 23, 26, 32, 34, 35, 43
Africa 17, 18, 21, 25, **27**, 28, 30, 34, 43
Angola 25
Aquino, Corazan 26
Argentina 12, 13, 36
armaments 13, **13**, 43
Asia 18, 29

Baker Plan 34–5
banks 6, 8, 9, 12, **12**, 14, **14**, 20, **20**, 32–3, 35, 37, 40
Bolivia 36, 38
Brazil 12, 13, 20, 21, **21**, 22, **22**, 23, 36, 39, **40**
Bremen, East Germany 16
Britain 41, 43

Cartagena, Colombia 36
cash crops 28, 30
Castro, Fidel 38, **38**
Chile 12, **18**, 21, 36
Citicorp 20, 40
Club of Paris, 33, 43
Colombia 36
colonialism 17
commodities 11, 37
copper **18**, 25
cotton **17**
Cuba 38
currency devaluation 22

debt equity swaps 36
default (on loans) 8, 12, 20
Depression 8, 30
developed countries 22, 40, 41
developing countries 6, 12, 17, 18, 19, 20, 22, 36, 39, 40, 43
Dominican Republic 36

Ecuador 36, 38
education 10, 22, 23, 24, 27
Edward I, 14
Edward III 14, **15**
EEC 43–4
environment 30, 43

Ethiopia **17**, **19**
exports 20, 22, 23, 25

famine 17
food 22, 24
  prices 25, 27, 36, 43
  production 23, 43
foreign currency 6, 22

Garcia, Alan 36, **36**
General Agreement on Tariffs and Trade (GATT) 18
Ghana 21
government aid 9, 10, 11, 41

health care 10, 21, 22, 24, 37
hunger 6, 8

imports 12, 20, 22
industrial production 8
inflation 23
International Development Administration (IDA) 19
International Monetary Fund (IMF) 19, 20, 22, 24, 25, 26, 32, 33, 34, 36, 37, 38, 43
interest 6, 10, 11, 12, 14, 18, 20, 32, 36, 41
international trade 8
Iranian revolution 11, **11**

Jamaica 21, 24–5, **24**, 27
Japan 14, 35–6, **35**, 43

Kaunda, Kenneth 25
Kenya **28**

Latin America 6, 8, 12, 18, 21, 24, 29, 34, 36, 38
Lawson, Nigel 43

malnutrition 26, 27
Manley, Michael 24
manufactured goods 18
manufacturing industries 11
Marcos, Ferdinanad 26
Marshall, George **17**
Marshall Plan 16
Mexico 12, 13, 20, 32, 36
moratorium 12, 13, 20, 32, 36, 39
Mozambique 25, 43

Niger 42
Nigeria 38
Nyerere, Julius 25

oil 11, 23
oil crisis 9

Peru 36–8, **36**
Philippines 26, **26**
poverty 6, 8, 14
public spending 22

quotas 18

raw materials 17, 18
rescheduling (of debts) 32, 34, 36

Seaga, Edward 25
shares 6, 8
Singapore **29**
social services 36, 43
Soviet Union 14, 43
subsidies 22, 23, 25, 27
Sudan 30, **31**
sugar 23
sugar beet 44
sugarcane 30
Tanzania 21
tariffs 8, 18

unemployment **7**, 8, **8**, 26, 36
UNICEF 43
United Nations Conference on Trade and Development (UNCTAD) 18
United States 6, **7** 8, 14, 16, 19, 41, 43
Uruguay 36

Venezuela 12, 13, 21, 36

Wall Street Crash 6, **7**, 30, 43
War on Want 41
Western countries 11, 20
Western governments 11, 19, 35, 40
World Bank 19, 24, 35, 36, 37, 43
World War I 30
World War II 16, 19, 30

Zambia 25, 25, **29**

47

DATE DUE			

336.3 D   Davies, Wendy.

The international debt crisis.

WITHDRAWN

Ferndale Area Elementary Library
100 Dartmouth Avenue
Johnstown, PA 15905

766653 56265A 06433E